TORONTO

PERCY ROWE

WORLD ALMANAC® LIBRARY

Please visit our web site at: www.worldalmanaclibrary.com
For a free color catalog describing World Almanac® Library's list of high-quality books
and multimedia programs, call 1-800-848-2928 (USA) or 1-800-387-3178 (Canada).
World Almanac® Library's fax: (414) 332-3567.

Library of Congress Cataloging-in-Publication Data

Rowe, Percy.
    Toronto / by Percy Rowe.
        p. cm. — (Great cities of the world)
    Includes bibliographical references and index.
    ISBN 0-8368-5026-2 (lib. bdg.)
    ISBN 0-8368-5186-2 (softcover)
    1. Toronto (Ont.)—Juvenile literature. [1. Toronto (Ont.)] I. Title. II. Series.
    F1059.5.T684R69   2003
    971.3'54—dc21   2003053477

First published in 2004 by
World Almanac® Library
330 West Olive Street, Suite 100
Milwaukee, WI 53212 USA

Copyright © 2004 by World Almanac® Library.

Produced by Discovery Books
Editor: Gianna Williams
Series designers: Laurie Shock, Keith Williams
Designer and page production: Keith Williams
Photo researcher: Rachel Tisdale
Maps and diagrams: Keith Williams
World Almanac® Library editorial direction: Jenette Donovan Guntly
World Almanac® Library editor: Jim Mezzanotte
World Almanac® Library art direction: Tammy Gruenewald
World Almanac® Library production: Beth Meinholz

Photo credits: Art Directors & Trip/A. Tovy: p.23; Art Directors & Trip/B. Turner: cover, title page, pp.34, 40; Art Directors &
Trip/S. Grant: p.37; Art Directors & Trip/T. Bognar: p.10; Chris Fairclough Photography: pp.5, 7, 13, 14, 16, 19, 20, 24, 25,
26, 27, 28, 33, 36, 42; Corbis/Bob Krist: p.17; Corbis/David G. Houser: p.39; Corbis/Duomo: p.38; Corbis/Gordon R.
Gainer: p.43; David Simson: pp.21, 31, 41; Hutchison Library/Robert Francis: pp.18, 30; Mary Evans Picture Library: pp.8,
11; Still Pictures/Martin Bond: pp.4, 32

Cover caption: The CN Tower is Toronto's signature, visible 30 miles (48 kilometers) away.
Two million paying visitors go up the tower each year.

Printed in the United States of America

1 2 3 4 5 6 7 8 9 07 06 05 04 03

Contents

Introduction

L ocated on the northwest shore of Lake Ontario, Toronto is Canada's largest city. In 1950, it was a quiet city of less than a million people, but its population has grown to five times that amount. Now the sixth largest North American city, it is still growing. Toronto, a vibrant, multi-ethnic metropolis, is a major economic and cultural center in Canada.

Toronto is the capital of Ontario, the most densely populated of Canada's ten provinces and three territories. Before Canada became a nation in 1867, Toronto, Montreal, and Kingston competed to be the Canadian capital. A small lumbering town called Ottawa was chosen as a compromise.

◄ *Toronto's skyline is crowded with skyscrapers built within the last fifty years, a mark of the city's growth.*

A Desirable Place to Live

The United Nations has often picked Canada as the most desirable country in the world in which to live. In terms of physical size, Canada is the world's second largest nation, behind Russia. The Canadian government is a constitutional monarchy—it consists of Parliament, made up of elected representatives, and a monarch with no real power. Canada's monarch, Elizabeth II, is also Great Britain's monarch. The prime minister, who is the leader of the political party with the most seats in Parliament, heads the Canadian government in Ottawa.

City of Neighborhoods

Toronto is built on relatively flat land, with several creeks and the shallow Humber and

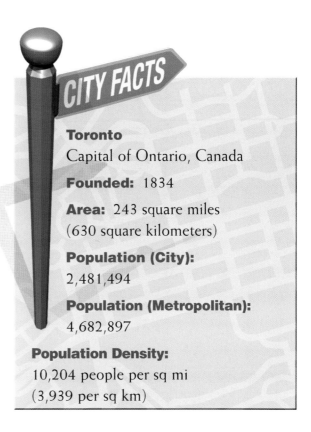

CITY FACTS

Toronto
Capital of Ontario, Canada

Founded: 1834

Area: 243 square miles (630 square kilometers)

Population (City): 2,481,494

Population (Metropolitan): 4,682,897

Population Density: 10,204 people per sq mi (3,939 per sq km)

Don Rivers all emptying into Lake Ontario, the fourth largest of the Great Lakes. Nicknamed the "City of Neighborhoods," Toronto has many residential areas beyond the central business district, with blocks of

▼ *The best place to view the Toronto skyline is from one of the city's island parks after a ferry ride.*

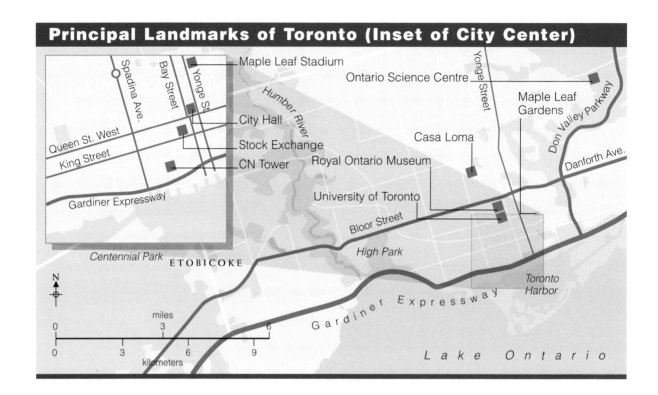

Principal Landmarks of Toronto (Inset of City Center)

Maple Leaf Stadium

Spadina Ave.

Bay Street

Yonge St.

Ontario Science Centre

Yonge Street

Maple Leaf Gardens

Don Valley Parkway

Humber River

City Hall

Queen St. West

King Street

Stock Exchange

CN Tower

Casa Loma

Royal Ontario Museum

Danforth Ave.

Gardiner Expressway

University of Toronto

Bloor Street

Centennial Park   ETOBICOKE

High Park

Toronto Harbor

N

miles

0   3   6

0   3   6   9

kilometers

Gardiner Expressway

Lake Ontario

apartment towers and sections of smaller homes mixed together. Toronto is a "green" city—along with tree-lined streets, it has many gardens and parks, including island parks in the middle of its rivers.

The central part of Toronto is box-shaped and bordered by highways. The Don Valley Parkway skirts the east and Highway 427 runs to the west. Highway 401 is to the north; the Gardiner Expressway runs along Lake Ontario to the south.

Splitting the "box" is Yonge Street, which runs north from Lake Ontario. Once an Indian trail, it is known as the "longest street in North America" because it ends 1,000 miles (1,600 kilometers) away, at the border of Ontario and Manitoba Provinces.

The downtown core of this box—the business heart of Canada—consists of sky-scrapers that are up to seventy-two stories high. This part of the city contains two major landmarks—the Canadian National (CN) Tower and the Skydome sports arena.

The Golden Horseshoe

The Greater Toronto Area (GTA) is part of the "Golden Horseshoe." From the city of Oshawa (a major center of auto manufacturing), this region extends eastward about 100 miles (160 km) along Lake Ontario, ending at Niagara Falls. The GTA stretches 40 miles (64 km) east to west and 12 miles (19 km) north to south, and it contains one quarter of the Canadian population.

King of the Clouds

The Canadian National Tower (right)—named for the railroad company that built it—dominates the Toronto skyline. The CN Tower is 1,815.5 feet (550 meters) high, but in summer, when heat makes it expand, it is 2 inches (5 centimeters) higher. In 1975, when the tower's antenna was lowered by helicopter, all of Toronto stopped to watch the completion of this unique landmark. Streetcars, buses, and cars were abandoned, and people cheered.

The world's tallest "free-standing structure," the tower provides an amazing 60-mile (100-km) view on clear days. Two million visitors a year board glass elevators that take less than a minute to reach the 1,450-ft (440-m) high Skypod, with its main viewing platforms, glass floor, and revolving restaurant. Many people have walked or run up the tower's 2,570 steps for charitable causes.

The Seasons of Toronto

Like many places in Canada, Toronto experiences long, snowy winters, averaging six major snowfalls a year. Toronto's winter temperatures, however, are usually somewhat warmer than Montreal, Ottawa, and cities on Canada's plains. Spring is short and cool, with freezing temperatures liable to occur until the middle of May. Summer is hot and often humid, while autumn is marked by colorful foliage.

CHAPTER 1

History of Toronto

The name Toronto means "gathering place" in the language of the Hurons (Wyandots), a Native American people. For centuries before European settlers arrived, the Hurons lived at the mouth of the Humber River on Lake Ontario. This area was the beginning of a canoe route to Lake Huron.

European Settlement

A French fur trader named Etienne Brûlé was the first European to visit the area, arriving in 1615. In the 1750s, a small store was built, followed by the establishment of Fort Rouillé. The fort was burned down in 1759 by French soldiers fleeing from invading British troops. The British then bought the area from the Hurons.

Loyal to Britain

Before the American Revolution, the area saw very little growth. After the war, however, "United Empire Loyalists"—people from the former American colonies who were still loyal to the British—began settling on the northern shore of Lake Ontario.

These settlements eventually became Upper Canada (present-day Ontario). The first governor of Upper Canada, James Graves Simcoe, chose Newark (present-day Niagara-on-the-Lake) as the capital, but the site had a major disadvantage—it was only a

◀ *This illustration shows Canadian refugees fleeing after York (now Toronto) was burned down by American invaders.*

September 14: "To see a Birch Canoe . . .
managed with that inexpressible ease &
composure which is the characteristic of an
Indian is the prettiest sight imaginable."

January 14: "There is a great deal of Snow
. . . on the River . . . which is so well frozen
that we walked some miles upon it. Near the
river we saw the track of Wolves. . . ."

March 4. "Though I wore 3 fur tippets
[gloves] I was so cold that I could hardly hold
My . . . cards this evening. This is the first
time we have felt the want of a Ceiling. . . ."

—The diary of Lady Elizabeth Simcoe, wife of
the first governor, written in 1793–94.

half mile from the new American republic. In 1793, Simcoe moved the capital to the site that would eventually become Toronto, naming it York. A fort was built at York, which was also a base for ships.

The War of 1812

By 1812, York had only seven hundred residents. At the time, tensions between British Canada and the United States were high. The United States believed the British were supporting Indian raids. In addition, the British were preventing U.S. ships from sending goods to France, which was at war with Britain. British sailors were also boarding U.S. ships in search of British deserters, and they often took U.S. sailors to serve on British ships.

The War of 1812 (1812–1814) began when the United States retaliated by invading British Canada. One important battle of the war—the Battle of Queenston Heights—took place near Niagara Falls. During this battle, an army led by British general Sir Isaac Brock defeated invading U.S. troops. Brock, who was killed in the battle, became one of Canada's heroes. Despite this victory, U.S. forces repeatedly invaded Upper Canada and, in 1813, captured York and destroyed many of its buildings. Four months later, however, British troops captured Washington, D.C., and burned down the Capitol building. The war ended in stalemate with a peace treaty.

Postwar Expansion

After the War of 1812, the British sought to make York less vulnerable to attack. They created a strong fort at York, even as the threat of U.S. invasion lessened. With peace restored, York's commercial activity began to grow. In the decades following the war, new settlers from Britain flooded into York and other regions in Upper Canada, buying land and establishing businesses.

The new settlers all had to contend with the "Family Compact." This group of wealthy, powerful men, many of whom belonged to the same family, controlled Upper Canada's government. Holding most political offices, they dominated the legisla-tive and executive bodies of Upper Canada. Most members were Anglicans who exerted a strong influence on religion and other aspects of Canadian life. They became rich through land grants, and they blocked all moves toward democracy.

Casa Loma

A well-known landmark in Toronto is Casa Loma (below), or "House on the Hill." Sir Henry Pellat, a businessman who made his fortune providing electricity in Canada, began construction of Casa Loma in 1911. Meant to resemble a medieval European castle, Casa Loma was built with gold-plated faucets, an indoor swimming pool, and a tunnel to nearby stables. Today, the castle is a popular tourist attraction.

Toronto's First Mayor

In 1834, York, with nine thousand inhabi-tants, became the city of Toronto. The city's first mayor was William Lyon Mackenzie, the hot-headed printer of a newspaper called the *Daily Colonist*. The paper spoke out against the Family Compact for

▲ *This nineteenth-century illustration depicts*
King Street, Toronto's main avenue in the 1880s.

not allowing elections. In 1837, he led a march in rebellion against them and was forced to flee to the United States. He returned in 1849, however, when government reforms were successful, and served eight years in the Upper Canada legislature.

New Settlers, New Nation

The immigrant flow from Britain continued, especially from Scotland, where many had lost their farms, and from Ireland, which experienced a potato famine from 1845 to 1848. The amount of immigrants grew with the coming of the railroad to Toronto in 1853. Before the railroad, the city's most important transportation route had been across Lake Huron (stagecoach service between Toronto and Montreal was also available). The railroad replaced the lake as the primary transportation route in and out of Toronto, and, because it ran along the lake, it also created a barrier between the

"The country around this town, being very flat, is bare of scenic interest. But the town is full of life and motion, bustle, business, and improvement. The streets are well paved, and lighted with gas; the houses are large and good; the shops excellent."

—Charles Dickens, British author, 1842.

11

"It is now to Toronto, rather than Winnipeg,

that the immigrant goes in large numbers,

be he German, Italian, Dutch, English, Polish,

Ukrainian or Hungarian. It is here that work

is to be found. It is here that 'streets are

paved with gold.'"

—From *The Times* of London, 1961.

city and the waterfront. Expansion of railroads across Canada helped Toronto become the main manufacturing supplier for western Canada, particularly of agricultural machinery, household goods, and hardware. In 1867, Upper Canada joined Lower Canada (modern-day Quebec) and some provinces on the Atlantic Coast to become the modern-day nation of Canada.

Education and Other Improvements
During the nineteenth century, facilities and services in Toronto grew. While controlled by the Family Compact, Toronto only had grammar schools for boys, which required students to pay a fee. Egerton Ryerson, an Anglican turned Methodist, helped establish a free, public elementary-school system and became Toronto's first superintendent of schools. Ryerson sought to establish nonsectarian schools, but Catholic schools became common in the 1850s. King's College opened its doors in 1843 but only to Anglicans. In 1850, however, the college

became the nonsectarian University of Toronto. In its first few decades, the school had no female students, mostly because few girls received early schooling.

In 1899, the population of Toronto—200,000—was still small compared with other Canadian cities. By then, however, the city boasted a children's hospital (now world-renowned), a library system, and a symphony orchestra, and it was also hosting the annual Canadian National Exhibition, a large fair that is still held today.

Changes in Immigration
Until 1950, Toronto was largely "WASP"—White, Anglo-Saxon, and Protestant. Immigrants to Toronto were mostly from Britain. Although most Irish settlers were Catholic, settlers from England and Scotland were Protestant. All of the settlers spoke English.

In the 1950s, however, up to a quarter of a million immigrants from other parts of the world began pouring into Canada each year, with half of them settling in the GTA. At first, many immigrants were from Europe, which had been ravaged by World War II. During the 1950s and 1960s, they came mainly from countries on the Mediterranean Sea, such as Italy. During the 1970s, immigrants flowed in from countries in the Caribbean Sea, and in the 1980s and 1990s they came from Asia. Recently, many refugees from Afghanistan, Somalia, the Middle East, and the former Yugoslavia have all settled in Toronto.

Sunday Laws

Toronto has a history of enforcing restrictions on Sunday, the Christian sabbath. Shopping on Sunday was not allowed in Toronto until 1992, and until World War II, stores also had to draw curtains across their window displays. Sporting events and movies were not permitted on Sundays until the 1960s. Toronto's strict moral code—of which the Sunday laws were a part—earned the city the nickname "Toronto the Good."

With this new immigration, the character of Toronto changed. A large Italian community developed, for example, with many Italians working as stonemasons and carpenters to help build the expanding city. Later, other immigrant communities also grew in Toronto, and the sights, smells, and sounds of many different cultures mixed together.

A Building Boom

As Toronto grew, large areas of farmland around the city became suburbs, and highways were built to bring workers to downtown jobs. Until the 1960s, however, the city lacked a vibrant "heart." Then Toronto's first Jewish mayor, Nathan Phillips, pushed for a new city hall and central square. The Finnish architect Viljo Revell created a daring design that gained worldwide attention. Once the City Hall opened, in 1965, skyscrapers began sprouting up around it.

Toronto has, however, suffered some setbacks. The St. Lawrence Seaway, completed in 1959, allowed oceangoing ships into the Great Lakes and was expected to make Toronto a major port. Despite improvements to the city's harbor, however, Toronto has not been able to compete with Halifax and St. John, Canadian ports that are free of ice all year. By 2001, Toronto's port areas had become a wasteland.

▼ *Today, the St. Lawrence Seaway is used almost exclusively by ships that only travel on the Great Lakes. Visits by oceangoing ships are rare.*

CHAPTER 2

People of Toronto

Today, almost two million people who live in Toronto were born in another country. With so many immigrants from all over the world, Toronto has become largely defined by its ethnic diversity. Many cultures co-exist in Toronto, and the city is proud of its racial and ethnic tolerance.

Forty-two percent of the immigrants arriving in Canada have chosen to live in the Greater Toronto Area. Ethnic minorities account for 40 percent of the population, compared with 11 percent nationwide. The largest ethnic minorities in Toronto today come from China, Italy, South Asia, and islands in the Caribbean.

Despite Toronto's considerable diversity, two minorities—French-Canadians and Native Americans—are almost nonexistent. Canada is bilingual, with English and French both official languages, but French-Canadians in the GTA form less than 1 percent of the population. Native Americans (known in Canada as First Nations people) are even more rare.

Towns within a City

Fifty years ago, Toronto had one small community of Chinese immigrants, known as Chinatown. Today, the city has a large, central Asiatown and four more Asian communities in the suburbs. The Asiatown in the heart of the city is centered around down-

◄ Pedestrians cross a downtown street, their faces reflecting the variety of nationalities that live in Toronto.

town Spadina Avenue. This area features tall, sculpted Chinese figures in traditional red and gold beside streetcar tracks. These colors are repeated on the exteriors of large Chinese restaurants, many of which have sculpted dragons and other figures at their entrances. Sidewalks are congested with stalls selling fresh fish and exotic, imported vegetables and fruit, such as a sour-smelling fruit called durian. The area also boasts a cinema complex showing Chinese movies, an indoor mall, and many other stores that sell Asian arts and crafts, silks, and kitchenware. In the 1940s, Central Technical Collegiate was known as the "Jewish school" because of the academic excellence of its Jewish students, but now it is called the "Chinese school" for Chinese students' record of academic achievement.

Cultural Pride

Although the children of immigrants usually

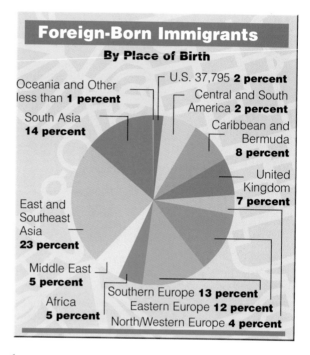

become part of a mainstream culture in Toronto, they also have opportunities to nurture their own native cultures. Students often attend weekend "heritage classes" to learn the language of their parents, and the city's summer festivals have pavilions featuring the

▲ *Toronto's largest Presbyterian church, Saint Andrew's, is now dwarfed by nearby skyscrapers.*

food, crafts, music, and dance of different countries. In addition, the Canadian government provides financial support to multilanguage radio and TV stations.

Religion

Toronto's ethnic diversity is reflected in the variety of its religious institutions. Roman Catholicism is now Toronto's largest religion, but the presence of other religions has increased markedly. The GTA also has thirty mosques where Muslims worship, as well as many Hindu temples in the suburbs. The Korean Christian Church has acquired the sites of several former Protestant churches and converted them.

Downtown Toronto has several churches where people of various Christian faiths can worship—St. James' Cathedral (Anglican), St. Michael's Cathedral (Catholic), St. Andrew's Church (Presbyterian), and the Metropolitan Church of the United Church. All of these churches have been surpassed in size by newcomers such as a Sikh temple near the city's airport. This Sikh temple is second in size only to the famed Golden Temple of Amritsar, India.

Two synagogues, Holy Blossom and Beth Tzedec, have been part of the city's main Jewish community in north Toronto for decades. Newer religious buildings, such as St. Mark's Coptic Orthodox Church in Scarborough (the North American headquarters for the Coptic Orthodox faith), have been built on the fringes of the city.

Secular Celebrations

Boxing Day (the day after Christmas) is the busiest day of the year for retail stores in Toronto. The day after Labor Day (the first Tuesday in September) is back-to-school day for children after nine weeks of summer vacation. Canadian Thanksgiving (held on the second Monday of October) is a low-key family occasion featuring many foods associated with Thanksgiving in the United States—turkey, cranberry sauce, and pumpkin pie. For Toronto residents, this holiday is the time for closing down lakeside cottages for winter.

Toronto residents also observe a Canadian holiday honoring a former queen. Called Queen Victoria's Birthday and held on May 24, the holiday marks the time for opening summer cottages and planting gardens.

Holidays and Festivals

Regardless of religious faith, most Toronto residents know about certain major religious holidays such as Ramadan (celebrated by Muslims) and Yom Kippur (a Jewish holiday). People of all faiths turn out to see the Hindu Diwali (Festival of Light) parade through the city's streets. Many people also attend Chinese New Year celebrations, which are held at a large exhibition hall on the Canadian National Exhibition grounds. These celebrations feature lion dances, acrobatics, martial arts displays, food, crafts, and fashion shows

Christmas is the most widely observed holiday in Toronto, and the Santa Claus parade held in November is a favorite among families. Like most Canadians, Toronto residents also take off Boxing Day, a traditional British holiday observed the day after Christmas (the name comes from "Christmas boxes," or presents). Another popular event is the Good Friday parade

▼ *The Caribana festival includes Toronto's largest parade, which sometimes lasts for eight hours.*

through Toronto's Italian community, Little Italy, which brings out thousands of spectators. Huge crowds also attend Caribana, the largest Caribbean festival in North America.

Changing Times, Changing Meals

The eating habits of Toronto's residents have changed in the last few decades. Sunday dinners featuring British-style roast beef have largely disappeared, for example, and Toronto now has a number of fast-food options for those who do not have the time or the energy to cook at home. In fact, Toronto can actually claim a connection to

▲ Crabs are for sale at an outdoor street market on Spadina Avenue, the main thoroughfare in Toronto's Asiatown.

a popular chain of stores—Tim Hortons— that sells coffee and baked goods in both Canada and the United States. The chain was started by Tim Horton, a hockey star who played for the Toronto Maple Leafs.

Ethnic Variety

Fast food is hardly the only dining choice available to the people of Toronto, who often eat out many times a week. The city's

▲ *Street vendors are always outside sports venues selling hotdogs and hamburgers, in all weather.*

ethnic diversity has resulted in a dizzying variety of restaurants offering every kind of cuisine. Toronto has numerous Italian, Chinese, Indian, and Vietnamese restaurants, as well as Thai spots and sushi bars. The Danforth is a long street of Greek restaurants. The city also boasts Ethiopian, Malaysian, Arabic, and Peruvian restaurants.

In addition to many ethnic restaurants, Toronto has a rich variety of ethnic specialty stores selling all kinds of exotic goods. Asian, Indian, and Caribbean stores, for example, can be found throughout the GTA. Indian stores sell special spices, Jamaican shops offer jerked pork, and whole city blocks are filled with stores specializing in Korean foods. Toronto's supermarkets also provide a a variety of ethnic foods, offering everything from Thai sauces to bok choy, a Chinese vegetable.

Fresh Food

Canada has many areas of fertile farmland and abundant supplies of seafood, such as fish and shellfish. Toronto residents enjoy a bountiful selection of high-quality produce, meats, and seafood as a result. Peaches, apricots, and plums arrive from the "fruit belt" along the Niagara River. Wild blueberries, cherries from British Columbia, apples, tomatoes, corn on the cob, and maple syrup are all readily available, along with beef from Alberta and pork, salmon, and shellfish. During Canada's cold winters, much food is imported from the United States.

A British Leftover

There are five hundred-seat banquet halls for weddings and anniversaries in Toronto. The city's most traditionally British building, the Old Mill, is also the city's most popular site. Built in the Tudor style of five hundred years ago, couples waltz to a live orchestra in the Old Mill's historic restaurant. Best of all, the establishment offers traditional English tea.

CHAPTER 3

Living in Toronto

Over the last fifty years, housing for the majority of people in the Greater Toronto Area has changed significantly. Until the 1950s, most people in Toronto lived in houses. Land for development outside Toronto was cheap, however, so housing prices and property taxes were lower than in the city. People started moving to less expensive suburban housing such as rented apartments and bought condominiums, or condos, which are apartments within a building that require an annual fee for upkeep.

Gradually, Toronto's adjoining cities, like Markham (20 percent of its population was born in China) and Mississauga, both part of the GTA, spread farther outward. Some commuters now travel two hours to get to work, while the average one-way car commute is fifty minutes. Moreover, a recent survey showed that there are now as many cars traveling out of the city in the morning rush-hour as into it, because offices and factories have relocated to the city's fringes—such as pharmaceutical giant GlaxoSmithKline Inc.'s huge plant to the western edge. Many families own two or three cars. Many sixteen-year-olds take their driving tests and get a secondhand car to drive to their part-time work while still at school, adding to the traffic congestion.

◀ *Some of Toronto's most expensive housing has been built facing the harbor on Queen's Quay.*

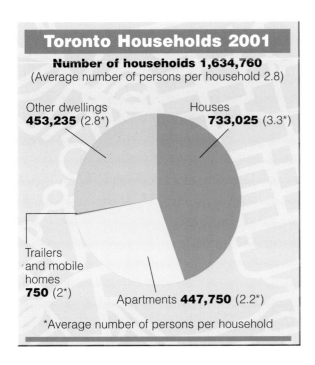

Toronto Households 2001

Number of households 1,634,760
(Average number of persons per household 2.8)

Other dwellings
453,235 (2.8*)

Houses
733,025 (3.3*)

Trailers
and mobile
homes
750 (2*)

Apartments **447,750** (2.2*)

*Average number of persons per household

▼ *Toronto's suburbs are lined with houses and often have wide, tree-lined sidewalks.*

Rich and Poor

As elsewhere in North America, the gap between rich and poor has grown over the past few decades. Less than 1 percent of apartment buildings and row houses are subsidized by the government to ensure low rents for poor people. The wealthy build ever bigger homes, some costing as much as $15 million. For the middle classes, houses are on roads still quiet enough for "shinny" (street hockey).

Suburban Life

Newcomers, in the past, generally had little money, so they first headed for the homes of relatives living in specific areas, usually neighborhoods that were overwhelmingly of one nationality. Little Italy is the best example of this sort of area.

Today, many immigrants arriving in the country have the money for a down payment on a house. Instead of first living in small downtown homes, they can buy large new houses on what was previously farmland. In "the 905"—another name for the GTA, derived from the area code—houses, malls, parks, and factories have all been built in the past thirty years.

Only a few buildings are unique, like the Lego-like Mississauga Civic Centre. In Centennial Park, the garbage of Etobicoke (a city now incorporated into Toronto) was used to create a ski hill. In Mississauga, the local symphony orchestra and choir present operas in its Living Arts Centre, which has a stage as large as any downtown theater.

Though the suburbs have expanded, there also has been a return to the city. With children grown up, couples move back into condos (one has butlers serving breakfast in bed daily), "renos" (made-over older homes), or high-ceilinged lofts in former factories.

Suburban Shopping

Suburban malls have proved an irresistible lure for city shoppers. The "big box" Walmart, Office Depot, Home Depot, and Toys 'R' Us stores—named for their one-story box shape—combined with free parking act as magnets, drawing customers away from the city center.

Each large suburb of Toronto has covered malls with up to sixty shops. The indoor mall—Sherway Gardens in Etobicoke, Square One in Mississauga, Yorkdale in north Toronto, and many others—is the modern shopper's mecca. Each has a Sears, Bay (Hudson's Bay Company), or lower-priced Zellers, or all three of these department stores; often a branch of the grocery chains like Loblaw's and Dominion Stores; a food court; a newsstand selling lottery tickets; a government-run liquor store; and dozens of shops.

Shopping in Town

For those who prefer bright lights and busy streets, central Toronto has four principal shopping areas at its heart. The Eaton Centre covers an entire block along Yonge Street. It consists of one hundred stores on three levels and was Canada's most visited tourist attraction during the 1990s.

Started in 1973, the Path, an underground pedestrian route, links 16 miles

Honest Ed's

"Honest Ed" Mervish helped in his parents' tiny corner store, then opened Honest Ed's, the largest discount store in Canada. A block long, it is covered with garish lights and silly signs that amusingly insult its owner. Ed, as everybody calls him, gives away hundreds of turkeys to poor people each Christmas and celebrates his birthday with bands, clowns, cake, and soda for all on a street named Mervish Village.

▲ *Overhead and underground walkways link the Eaton Centre to many other attractions.*

(27 km) of shops, food outlets, businesses, and entertainment venues. It stretches from the main bus depot to the CN Tower.

Bloor Street and Yorkville is a rich, two-block stretch consisting of one of the city's main east-west streets with, behind it, two parallel narrow roads, making up the Yorkville area. Thirty years ago, entertainers such as Harry Belafonte, Bill Cosby, and Joni Mitchell sometimes performed in its coffee houses, which have now been replaced by specialty boutiques. Lastly, Queen Street West is a four-block, young shopper's favorite because of its fashionable clothes.

Markets and Supermarkets

Weekly food shopping in Toronto is in supermarkets, some with service shops for photography, drugs, shoe repairs, and cleaning. The indoor downtown St. Lawrence Market is a weekend social center for many who stop to gossip with friends over coffee and peameal bacon-on-a-bun breakfasts while shopping. (The bacon is pickled, then dusted with corn meal.) Kensington Market is a year-round outdoor/indoor market, with lower prices. There is also an indoor antiques market at the lakefront, open seven days a week. A large waterside warehouse nearby has been converted into chic shops and restaurants; it's a favorite of summer tourists.

Education in Toronto

The realities of modern-day living have affected family life in Toronto as much as anywhere in the developed world. While parents work, children are often in day-care centers at age three and in kindergarten at five.

Students start school at 8.30 A.M. and the day ends at 3.30 PM. The number of pupils in the average class is about twenty-five. Except in private schools, students do not wear uniforms. Toronto's children attend primary school from first grade through eighth and high school from ninth through twelfth. Starting in first grade, some children learn all subjects in French, Canada's second language. All other students must take one year of French. Here, as in every aspect of Toronto life, immigration has made an indelible mark: 41 percent of public-school students speak a language other than English as their first language.

Private and Religious Schools

Only 4 percent of students go to private schools. There are 553 public schools, plus 211 Catholic schools, in the city proper. Their curricula, set by the province, are the same, except there is religious instruction in Catholic schools.

There are also Jewish and Muslim schools, although most Jewish and Muslim children attend public schools. Muslim schools are attached to mosques; the central Jami Mosque offers the most programs.

Universities

To graduate from high school, a student needs thirty credits, with one year's compulsory French, and math and English as compulsory subjects for four years. Six extra Ontario Academic Credits (OAC) are needed to enter a university, plus a grade point average of 75 percent for the more select schools. The brightest children, with a grade point nearer to 90 percent, can get into the University of Toronto. Toronto's other two universities, York and Ryerson, require a grade point average of about 80 percent. Several community colleges offer diplomas in everything from physical therapy to horticulture, from horse management to cooking.

After School

Few sports are played at school so most students are home by 4:00 PM for

▶ *Yellow school buses, bringing students in from out of town, are a common sight in the city.*

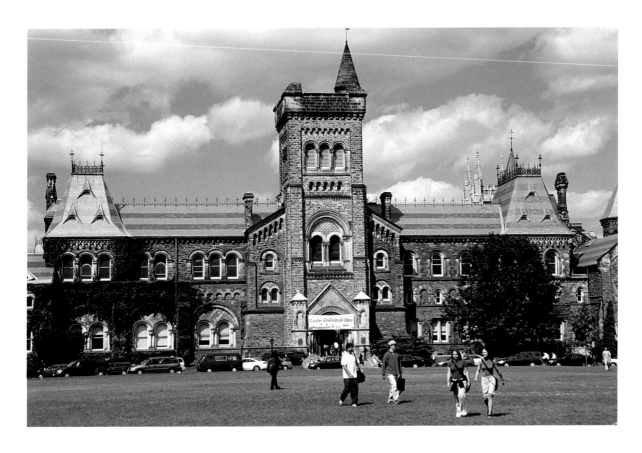

▲ *University College is at the heart of the University of Toronto, which consists of scores of buildings— some in suburbs 20 miles (32 km) from downtown.*

video games, to watch TV programs like *The Simpsons*, and do homework on computers (more than half of Toronto homes have a computer). Until they are fourteen, more children play soccer than hockey, but then they switch to hockey, baseball, and Canadian football played in leagues on rented arena rinks or in parks. In winter, snowboarding has become more popular than skiing. Nearly all high schoolers work during the summer vacation, often as lawn cutters, pool lifeguards, babysitters, and at store checkout counters.

Inner-City Problems

Toronto has never had a race riot, a major political scandal, a terrorist explosion, nor any record of police violence. The crime rate has dropped markedly since the early 1990s. Canada has strict gun laws. The homicide rate in Toronto is one-tenth what it is in many major U.S. cities.

Nevertheless, being a big city and growing bigger, there are problems. Crimes that now receive the most attention are white collar crimes, involving illegal stock trading

25

A Bleak Picture

Homelessness has soared in the past decade. The majority of the homeless population of Toronto are poor and jobless. A quarter of them are young men. Many come to Toronto from smaller towns. To care for them, the city has created social service agencies such as the Salvation Army, Food Bank, and Out of the Cold.

Today there are sixty-two shelters where homeless people can get food and a bed. Most places can hold twenty people, but the Salvation Army has shelters for two hundred. In extreme cold, vans circulate among the homeless, distributing hot beverages and blankets.

Food Bank distributes food received from stores. Out of the Cold provides hot meals, mats for sleeping, showers, and free haircuts, mainly in church halls, but also in university buildings and Osgoode Hall, home of the Ontario Law Society. Volunteers do 90 percent of the work.

or embezzlement. In addition, anti-Semitic graffiti and damage to synagogues in the Jewish communities of northern Toronto has been seen. Gang warfare has also increased, and several drug-driven homicides in or near nightclubs have prompted an all-out police drive to round up guns. This comes at a time when all gun owners across Canada are being ordered to register their firearms or face fines or jail.

While there have been occasional large seizures of drugs and convictions of traffickers, most people are being charged for possession of small amounts. Marijuana use is being allowed for medical treatment, particularly for AIDS patients.

Health Threats

Smog, water pollution, and a lack of electricity are all summer problems in Toronto. On hot, high "smog index" days, warnings are issued for those with breathing problems to stay indoors in air-conditioned homes. Air-conditioning peaks strain electricity supplies and brownouts (temporary power outages) are likely if demand grows unless new costly generators are built. In 2002, despite car emission controls in many U.S. states and Canadian provinces, pollution from traffic and industry resulted in twenty summer days when Torontonians with lung problems were advised to stay indoors. Pollution of the Great Lakes from the industrial waste of Buffalo, Niagara Falls, New York, Chicago, Detroit, other U.S. cities, and Canadian

▼ *While graffiti is not as common in Toronto as in other urban areas, a city department has been set up to combat it.*

effluents still result in the temporary closure of Toronto's beaches.

In spring 2003, Toronto was one of the first western cities to be struck by the mysterious SARS (Severe Acute Respiratory Syndrome) virus. By April, over three hundred people were sick with the virus and fourteen had died.

While these are all threats to health, Torontonians are generally fit and live as long as rural Canadians. They are covered by government health insurance except for dental and certain elective services. Many have their own insurance to cover drugs. Despite some delays in nonurgent surgery, polls repeatedly show the majority think their government-run health-care system works well.

CHAPTER 4

Toronto at Work

Until the 1970s, Montreal and Toronto each claimed to be Canada's commercial center. Now there is no doubt. With the worldwide growth of English as the language of business, Toronto has gained precedence over French-speaking Montreal. Many American companies have set up their branch headquarters in Toronto, while the headquarters of five national banks were already located there.

Four-fifths of all Canadian stock trading goes through the Toronto Exchange. Tax rates are moderate, although office space costs more than in Montreal. The city has three convention centers and a National Trade Centre for trade shows.

Toronto's Industries

Automobile building is Ontario's biggest industry. Though the assembly plants are in Oshawa and Oakville, on the edges of the GTA, numerous automotive parts factories (notably that of giant Magna International) are scattered throughout it, as are other plants for telecommunications, aircraft parts, and farm equipment. In addition, Toronto is Canada's center for book publishing, general printing, producing packaged foods, and for insurance and other financial services.

All of these industries have required office towers and (usually) giant one-story

◄ Toronto police use bicycles to patrol the more congested downtown streets.

factories on the outskirts, just as their workers have needed homes. This has meant an almost continuous building boom, making the construction industry a winner, as well.

A Worker's Lot

For decades, Toronto's construction employees have worked seventy and more hours a week in summer. Now work weeks of fifty to sixty hours are becoming more widespread in other occupations, especially for midlevel executives, owners of small stores, and others trying to make monthly payments on two cars, mortgages on large homes and lake cottages, and the costs of foreign vacations and expensive sports like skiing.

Unions are strong in the car industry, construction trades, and among civil servants, police officers, and teachers. However, there has been little headway in unionizing some jobs, especially those

Bay Street

The rest of Canada envies Toronto's wealth, and for decades it has been labeled "Hogtown." Bay Street, at the heart of the city's financial district, runs north from the Fairmont Royal York Hotel, once the largest hotel in the British Commonwealth. Surrounding Fairmont Royal York Hotel are towers, including First Canadian Place—the tallest—and Royal Bank Plaza, the walls of which glisten with gold leaf. They are filled with corporation lawyers, insurance companies, accountants, bank executives, and the Stock Exchange.

part-time positions in fast-food outlets, clothing, and other retail stores, usually held by young people who are often still in school. These workers are paid the minimum wage of less than $5.00 an hour.

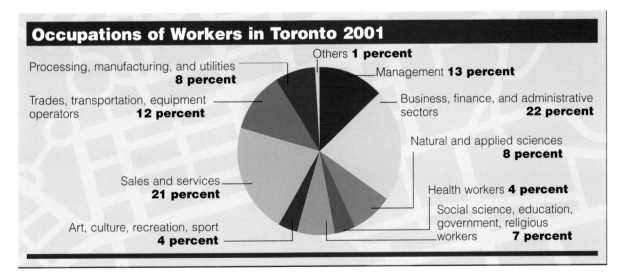

Occupations of Workers in Toronto 2001

- Processing, manufacturing, and utilities **8 percent**
- Trades, transportation, equipment operators **12 percent**
- Sales and services **21 percent**
- Art, culture, recreation, sport **4 percent**
- Others **1 percent**
- Management **13 percent**
- Business, finance, and administrative sectors **22 percent**
- Natural and applied sciences **8 percent**
- Health workers **4 percent**
- Social science, education, government, religious workers **7 percent**

▲ *The Fairmont Royal York Hotel faces the main railroad station and is within walking distance of the Metro Toronto Convention Centre.*

The Place to Visit

Hospitality and cultural industries in Toronto together make up an industry second only to manufacturing. It is estimated that 10 million tourists visit Toronto every year. For eight months of the year, thirty thousand hotel rooms serve business people and conventioneers. Overseas tourists crowd the rooms in the four warm weather months, when Americans from border states, partly drawn by the city's reputation for cleanliness and safety, also come for weekends. Many tourists cross the border for the huge Caribana parade, movie fans flock to the film festival, and the Gay Pride parade is also a big annual draw.

The city's George Brown Community College runs a first-class hospitality institute. Many of its graduates are chefs in top international hotels and on cruise ships.

"Toronto is the most undemonstrative city I know, and the least inquisitive. The Walkman might be made for it."

—Jan Morris, British travel writer.

A Media City

Toronto is the media capital of Canada. The Canadian Broadcasting Corporation's (CBC) English TV and radio services for the nation are located in the city, as is 70 percent of the Canadian film industry.

Twenty-five thousand people work in the TV and film industry, many for Hollywood producers who make movies in the city with stars like Harrison Ford and Whoopi Goldberg. Recent movies that have been made in Toronto include *Chicago*, *My Big Fat Greek Wedding* and *X-Men*.

There are five English-language newspapers in Toronto: the *Toronto Star* is Canada's biggest; the *Globe and Mail* and the *National Post* are national; the *Toronto Sun* is a tabloid; and the *Metro* is a free paper. There are also newspapers written in Chinese, Italian, German, and French.

Traffic Congestion

Traffic congestion is a problem in major cities around the world. Although costly expressways have been built to help suburban commuters get into town, no new arterial roads have been built in Toronto for forty years, and the downtown area is getting clogged. Many remedies have been suggested, including creating more bike lanes; lower bus, streetcar, and subway fares to attract more riders; express buses; or charging drivers a toll to enter downtown, a tactic that has cut congestion in other cities' busy areas considerably.

◄ *The* Globe and Mail *is a national paper, while the* Star *has Canada's largest circulation.*

Public Services

While private cars crowd the streets, Toronto's transit system has a reputation for safety, cleanliness, and punctuality. The first subway line opened in 1954. There are now seventy stations on three lines. Many ride the "red rockets"—Toronto's 248 streetcars—and buses. Toronto once had the largest number of streetcars in the world.

GO commuter trains—short for Government of Ontario—connect the suburbs with the central city. GO has lines running 60 miles (100 km) out of Toronto, especially west to Hamilton and east to Oshawa. In nonpeak hours, it runs buses on lesser-used routes. Taxi use is insignificant compared with, for example, New York City, but tourists in summer can take a rickshaw, usually pulled by an athletic student.

▼ *Double-decker GO trains bring suburban commuters into the city from Hamilton in the west and Oshawa in the east.*

▲ *Toronto has more streetcars than any other North American city. One route extends 20 miles (32 km).*

On the Water

Lake transportation includes all different kinds of boats, ranging from gondolas to tall ships, which cruise the harbor. Frequent ferries cross to the popular island parks, which face the city.

Although "lakers" are the only ships in the Port of Toronto, bringing in coal, grain, building materials, and salt for winter roads, the city is still a major transfer point, with large railyards, warehouses, and trucking centers.

Taking to the Air

Pearson Airport is the country's busiest airport. Now being rebuilt to take 30 million passengers a year, its present congestion is partly caused by Canadians flocking to resorts in Florida and the Caribbean in winter. There are daily flights to all major European capitals, many flights a day to major

U.S. and Canadian cities, and hourly flights to Ottawa and Montreal. Air cargo planes mainly arrive at night, with flowers from South America, and pharmaceuticals from Germany. Cattle are shipped out to Cuba. A small downtown airport, approached by the shortest ferry ride in Canada, is for short-distance aircraft.

Governing Toronto

Twelve municipalities surrounded Toronto until 1953. Then, a powerful politician, "Big Daddy" Fred Gardiner, masterminded a metropolitan government, the first in North America. Later, these municipalities were reshaped into five boroughs, then cities. Finally, in 1998, amalgamation created one big city, run by a mayor, and a councillor for each of forty-four wards.

The City Council

Council officials are elected for three-year terms. There are no political parties at this city level: each councillor is elected on the basis of his or her own political values. Interest in the workings of local government is low, and turnout for local elections is poor; often only 35 percent of the citizenry votes. After discussion in committees, final votes on issues are made in full council. The mayor has no power to veto.

A Memorable Mayor

The first mayor of the amalgamated metropolitan area of Toronto was Mel Lastman.

▼ *Toronto has two adjacent city halls. The new city hall (left) was planned to replace the old one (right), which is now used as a courthouse.*

Cleanliness

Actor Peter Ustinov defined Toronto as "New York designed by a Swiss." The phrase was inspired by a famous story. An American film crew who littered the street in imitation of a U.S. city returned from lunch only to find a city sanitation crew had picked up the garbage.

"Superman was conceived by Toronto-born Joe Shuster who originally worked not for the Daily Planet *but for* The Star, *modeled on the* Toronto Star. *This makes his assumed identity of bland Clark Kent . . . inevitable. Kent is the archetypical middle-class Toronto WASP, superficially nice, self effacing."*

—Mordecai Richler, Canadian novelist.

First elected in 1998, before the metropolitan government had been formed, Lastman was re-elected in November 2000. His flamboyant style and often badly worded social and political comments earned the millionaire the nickname "the tanned time bomb." All the same, Lastman has remained a popular figure in Toronto, with a reputation for getting the job done.

Running the City

It costs a great deal of money to run a city as large as Toronto. The metropolitan government's budget exceeds that of six of Canada's whole provinces. The Toronto City Council accomplishes its work by using a sytem of committees. These committees include representatives responsible for city functions such as policy and finance, administration, planning and transportation, economic development and parks, works, and community services.

All of these committees report to three other committees and the Board of Health.

These higher committees, in turn, report to the city council. In 2003, the council's committees were reviewed in the period before municipal elections were held that year.

Services

The Toronto metropolitan government runs the fire, ambulance, and water service, as well as other social services. The city also runs a unified police force of seven thousand officers through a board of five appointed civilian members (people who do not officially work for the police force), plus the mayor. There are, in addition, other forces of several thousand police officers who work in the border cities of the GTA. These officers work on foot, in boats, on horseback, and, most often, in patrol cars.

35

CHAPTER 5

Toronto at Play

There are plenty of things to do outside in Toronto. A series of parks, threaded by lagoons, forms an arc of thirteen islands protecting Toronto's harbor and are reachable only by ferry. Bicycles are the only vehicles allowed. The islands are especially popular with families for weekend picnics and games or visits to a children's farm or an amusement park.

The islands provide the best view of the city, looking back to Harborfront, a mile-long (1.6 km) waterfront combination of walks, yacht basins, street artists, stores, cafes, a model-boat pool, craft studios, two theaters, an art gallery, and an open stage for jazz and pop bands. It hosts four thousand events every year, and attracts 3 million visitors.

Ontario Place is a summer-only amusement center on artificial islands joined by glass-enclosed walkways. It includes an Imax theater, a children's water park, and the large Molson Centre for rock, rap, reggae, and hiphop artists.

City Parks

Of the thirty parks that have frontage on Lake Ontario, Sunnyside is the busiest, with in-line skaters, cyclists, joggers, walkers and—on the lake within a breakwater—rowers, canoeists, and boats shaped like dragons. Once an amusement park with

◀ *Regattas are held in the inner harbor, but there are also three-day races using the length of the lake.*

rides, its carousel is now at Disneyland in California.

Until recently, High Park was the city's largest green space, but a former midtown airport is being converted and will take the title. Even so, it will not be as large as the Toronto Metro Zoo on the city's outskirts.

Outdoor Festivals

Downtown, outdoor events include three jazz festivals, lasting from a weekend to ten days long; Grand Prix motor racing on

downtown streets one July weekend; a May weekend when the public can see the interior of historic buildings now in private use; and Canada Day fireworks.

▼ *Ontario Place, an entertainment center, is linked to the Canadian National Exhibition grounds by bridges.*

Cottage Living

Thousands of Torontonians have summer cottages for weekends and vacation on the Muskoka and Kawartha chains of lakes, two hours' drive north of the city. These are only a few of the 250,000 lakes in Ontario. On a per capita basis, Torontonians own more summer cottages than any other people in the world.

Sporting Chances

The most popular spectator sport in Toronto is hockey. For sixty years, there was never an empty seat in the seventeen thousand-seat Maple Leaf Gardens when Toronto's hockey team, the Maple Leafs, played a home game. Now that hockey is played in the larger Air Canada Centre, it is the same story there.

Torontonians also are avid supporters of the Raptors basketball team, while at the fifty-five thousand-seat Skydome they follow the Blue Jays, Toronto's baseball team, although now with only half-capacity crowds. These crowds are a long way from the sell-outs of the early 1990s when, for two years running, the Jays were World Series champions. The Skydome is also the home for the Argonauts. Unlike other sports teams, who all play against U.S. teams in U.S.-dominated leagues, the Argos play Canadian football only against other

◄ *Basketball wasn't a popular Toronto sport until the Raptors came to town with their star, Vince Carter.*

▲ *The Ontario Science Centre is built on a wooded ravine. One of its halls is devoted to space travel.*

Canadian city teams.

Average Torontonians enjoy snowboarding and both downhill and cross-country skiing, driving two hours north to winter resorts. Those at Collingwood on Lake Huron provide the best heights for skiing and views.

Indoor Fun

When the weather is bad, there are plenty of indoor attractions to keep Torontonians away from their couches. Fall in the city brings the first major indoor event—Toronto's ten-day Film Festival in September, now regarded as one of the world's top five. The following month it is the authors' turn. For twenty years, Torontonians have been turning out to hear writers—from spy novelist John LeCarre to Harry Potter's creator J.K. Rowling—read from their latest works.

The Ontario Science Centre is built in a valley so visitors go by escalators down a glass tunnel from the reception area to exhibition halls containing many hands-on exhibits on space, transportation, health, and chemistry.

Toronto Museums

The Royal Ontario Museum has displays ranging from armor to bats, but is best-known for having the largest collection of Chinese exhibits outside of China. Next door stands the Children's Own Museum, across the street is a Museum of Ceramics, and there are also museums devoted to shoes, sugar, and police work. None of these gets as many ardent young visitors as the Hockey Hall of Fame, nor are exhibits so well polished as the large Henry Moore sculptures, slid down by children outside the Art Gallery of Ontario (AGO). The AGO has the largest collection of the sculptor's work outside of his native Great Britain.

▲ *The Princess of Wales Theatre was built by impresario Ed Mervish for long-run mega-musicals.*

Dramatic Events

Toronto ranks third in the world for theaters after London and New York. Apart from six commercial theaters, each with more than one thousand seats, are a score of smaller theaters. Young People's Theatre puts on half a dozen productions each winter, and in May at Harborfront, the Milk Festival presents children's plays and puppetry.

Andrew Lloyd Webber musicals like *Cats* and Disney spectacles like *The Lion King* have had runs lasting years. Other shows try out in Toronto before going on to Broadway in New York City. Many of the smaller theaters present new Canadian plays. Some of these—*Two Pianos, Four Hands*, for one—go on to become Broadway hits.

Torontonians think nothing of driving 80 miles (130 km) to the theater, which is partly responsible for the success of the Stratford Shakespeare Festival. This little town sells 650,000 tickets to its twelve productions each May-November season. Now the biggest repertory theater in North America, it started in a tent with the famous actor Sir

Alec Guinness in a starring role. Little Niagara-on-the-Lake, near the Falls, has a population of only eight thousand, but boasts three theaters. The town sells 350,000 tickets each summer. It is the only place in the world to have an annual Shaw Festival for the plays of George Bernard Shaw. As well as these small towns, there are about twenty other Ontario "summer cottage towns," each with their own light theatrical shows.

Music Making

There is almost as much choice in music as in theaters. Apart from the Toronto Symphony Orchestra's long season in Roy Thomson Hall, the city's main concert venue, the Canadian Opera Company, presents half a dozen operas a season in a three thousand-seat theater. Much of its success is because there are translated "surtitles" above the stage so the audience can follow the plot. Toronto is also the home of the National Ballet Company of Canada, the Tafelmusik Orchestra, which is internationally known for its baroque music, and the Mendelssohn Choir, only one of a dozen choirs that present *The Messiah* during the Christmas season.

Nightclubs like The Docks can seat two thousand people to listen to lively music. Movies in multiplexes, with up to twenty-four movie theaters, help keep people entertained during the cold winter months.

▶ *This aerial view shows the unusual drum design of Roy Thomson Hall, the city's main concert hall.*

CHAPTER 6

Looking Forward

With crime decreasing markedly over the past ten years, no major religious or racial tensions, a particularly healthy economy since the start of the new century, and an assured influx of immigrants, few cities can feel so optimistic as Toronto.

Further Immigration

Appointed Canada's minister of immigration in 2002, Denis Coderre wants to increase immigration to Canada to 1 percent of the population per year. That would soon mean 350,000 newcomers annually, creating a bigger domestic market, and less reliance on exports to the United States. Although Coderre wants to steer newcomers away from major cities, huge numbers are still likely to come to Toronto, all wanting housing, furnishings, and cars. Employment in Toronto thus should continue to be high to satisfy these needs. The city's unemployment rate is about 3 percent, far lower than the national average of 7 percent.

Future Challenges

A growing population does, of course, create problems for cities. During the past five years, Toronto has been battling with the the provincial government in Ontario and

◀ Toronto has had a ten-year-long construction boom, following an influx of businesses into the city. The trend may soon slow for commercial building.

▲ The city of Toronto is extravagantly lit after dark. It is a busy place, known for its vibrant nightlife and tourist-friendly downtown area.

the federal government to get more money for social services, particularly for schools, hospitals, and public transportation.

Toronto lost to Beijing in a bid for the 2008 Summer Olympics. If it had won, the plan was to clean up the large polluted port area to build an Olympic Village, and reroute traffic through green space beside the lake. These plans are now in limbo.

Meanwhile, the latest of many traffic studies only suggests patchwork solutions. The main problem is that tens of thousands of cars in the city are carrying only one person. The subway system is efficient, but the number of suburban trains is few compared with cities like New York and London.

On the bright side, the Royal Ontario Museum and Art Gallery of Ontario are undergoing huge expansions. Toronto is also planning to build its first opera house by 2005, which will only strengthen its appeal to visitors from around the world.

Time Line

A.D. 1000–1700 The Huron Indians inhabit the area where the Humber River empties into Lake Ontario.

1615 Etienne Brûlé, a French fur trader, explores the Humber River.

1750–51 Fort Rouillé is built on the site of the present Canadian National Exhibition grounds; it burns in 1759.

1791 Upper Canada is created with John Graves Simcoe as its first governor. Two years later, York (now Toronto) is made the region's capital.

1813 York is burned in the War of 1812 between the British and Americans.

1834 York, with nine thousand people, becomes the city of Toronto.

1837 Former mayor William Mackenzie leads a rebellion against the powerful Family Compact.

1853 The first railroad comes to Toronto.

1867 The nation of Canada is born.

1949 Subway construction begins.

1953 Thirteen municipalities are put under Canada's first metropolitan government.

1959 The St. Lawrence Seaway is opened.

1961–67 The Toronto Maple Leafs win the Stanley Cup, the emblem of hockey supremacy, four times.

1967 Toronto is reorganized into the city itself and five boroughs.

1975 The CN Tower is completed.

1992–93 The Toronto Blue Jays win two World Series baseball titles back to back.

1998 Toronto becomes one city.

2003 Toronto is struck by Severe Acute Respiratory Syndrome (SARS) virus.

Glossary

amalgamation joining together; process that made five cities become one city of Toronto in 1998.

Anglicans members of the Protestant Church of England.

Anglo-Saxon pertaining to the Germanic people who lived in Britain in the fifth and sixth centuries.

baroque a musical style that was current between 1600 and 1750.

Catholic pertaining to the Roman Catholic church.

Commonwealth (British) an association between Britain and countries that were formerly part of the British Empire.

curricula programs that a school or school district sets for its pupils.

embezzlement stealing money that has been entrusted to one's care.

land grants parcels of land given to individuals or groups by the government.

metropolitan belonging to one of the chief cities of a country.

mortgages property loans.

municipalities towns that govern themselves.

nonsectarian not associated with a specific religious group.

Parliament place where elected officials make laws and govern a country.

per capita per person in the population.

Protestant member of a Christian church that is not under the jurisdiction of the Catholic church, and that does not recognize the Pope as its spiritual leader.

provinces the principal divisions of a country; similar to states in the U.S.

secular nonreligious.

subsidized partly or completely funded (said of a service).

synagogues Jewish places of worship.

unions organizations that represent workers in negotiations over their rights with employers.

wards smaller divisions of a large city that elect representatives to the city council.

WASP (White Anglo-Saxon Protestant) a member of the white upper-middle class.

Further Information

Books

Bowers, Vivien. *Only in Canada!: From the Colossal to Kooky*. Toronto, ON: Maple Tree Press, 2002.

Comeau, Natalie Ann, Christine Battuz, and Bob Kirner. *The Lobster Kid's Guide to Exploring Toronto*. Montreal, QU: Lobster Press Limited, 2000.

Goodman, Michael E. *Toronto Blue Jays*. Manatako, MN: The Creative Company, 2002.

Nichols, John. *Toronto Maple Leafs (Stanley Cup Champions)*. Manatako, MN: Creative Education, 2003.

Rogers, Barbara Radcliffe and Stillman D. Rogers. *Toronto (Cities of the World)*. San Francisco, CA: Children's Press, 2000.

Web Sites

www.torontotourism.com
Toronto-based events.

www.rom.on.ca
Royal Ontario Museum web site.

www.ago.net
Art Gallery of Ontario web site.

www.ontariosciencecentre.ca
Ontario Science Centre's web site.

bluejays.mlb.com/NASApp/mlb/index.jsp?c_id=tor
Toronto's baseball team's web site.

www.batashoemuseum.com
Museum of Footwear web site.

Index

Page numbers in **bold** indicate pictures.

J
971.3
Row

Rowe, Percy.

Toronto.